DAVE DC … -KE...

VIRGINIA A. ARNOLD

PICTURES BY
EUGENIE FERNANDES

MACMILLAN/McGRAW-HILL SCHOOL PUBLISHING COMPANY
New York Chicago Columbus

Dave does NOT like...
Swimming in waves,

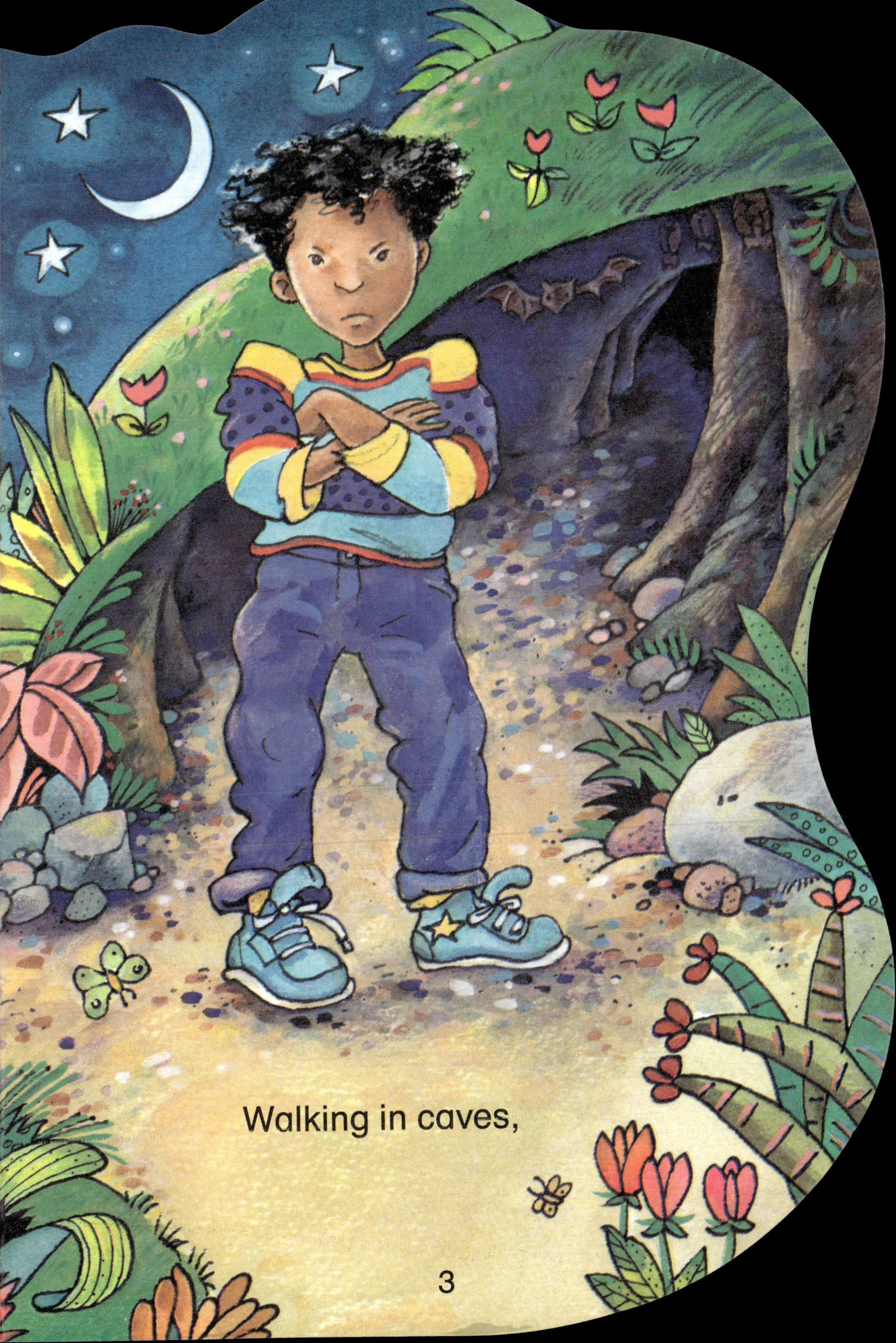

Walking in caves,

People who say,
"Now be brave, Dave!"

Dave DOES like...

A party Kay gave,

Watching Daddy shave,

Having people say,
"What a save, Dave!"